VB.NET AND
THE REGISTRY

In plain English

Richard Thomas Edwards

CONTENTS

Before we get started
Why am I writing this book?

There are very few people in the world more qualified to create a book off the top of their head about the registry than I am. I've been working with the registry since 1998. I've solved some tough issues as a Microsoft technical support specialist and know where to go in the registry when I want to gather information to resolve issues.

I also know that the registry isn't a place where you just start getting rid of keys, names and values. One wrong key removed, and you will be rebuilding your operating system.

Because of this reason, this book is about how to write registry programs that merely read the registry and glean information from it. Indeed, there isn't one piece of code in this book about removing, modifying or writing to the registry. Nor is there any discussion about how to do those kinds of things.

Since I don't like long introductions and want to dive into the world of the registry, let's get started talking about how the registry came about in the first place.

Two paragraphs on the history of the registry

Between 1970 and 1995, most programs relied on text files outside of the program to – also known as config or ini files – to provide continuity for program and user settings. How the program would work.

But when Microsoft started becoming the center of attention for users, programmers found themselves moving that information into something called the registry which provided them with, essentially, the same kind of support. Ever since then, the registry is the place where information about how a program should be configured.

In the beginning there were hives

Although it isn't clear how the word hives was used to describe the various sections of the registry – one story suggested the programmer who designed it hated bees and knew that if you changed one key you would get stung – it really doesn't matter. The fact is, to this day, each section is called a hive.

While there used to be more, in today's world, these hives are:

HKEY_CLASSES_ROOT
HKEY_CURRENT_CONFIG
HKEY_CURRENT_USER
HKEY_LOCAL_MACHINE
HKEY_USERS

Each one of these has its own special reason for existing. In fact, up until recently, HKEY_CLASSES_ROOT was where all the extensions and their associated executables and all the classes with all their associated appIDs, Interfaces and type Libraries were located.

Today, of course, that is not the case as HKEY_LOCAL_MACHINE has taken on the task of dealing with both 64-bit and 32-bit programs.

The image below will show you clearly a distinction between the world of 32-bit programs and 64-bit ones. The full path to get there is HKEY_LOCAL_MACHINE\Software

- **SOFTWARE**
  - ActiveState
  - AGEIA Technologies
  - Classes
  - Clients
  - Embarcadero
  - Khronos
  - Macromedia
  - Microsoft
  - Mozilla
  - mozilla.org
  - MozillaPlugins
  - NVIDIA Corporation
  - ODBC
  - Perl
  - Policies
  - RegisteredApplications
  - **Wow6432Node**
    - AGEIA Technologies
    - Classes
    - Clients
    - Embarcadero
    - Google
    - Khronos
    - Macromedia
    - Microsoft
    - MimarSinan
    - Mozilla
    - MozillaPlugins
    - Nuveen
    - NVIDIA Corporation
    - ODBC
    - Policies
    - Python
    - RegisteredApplications
    - RubyInstaller
    - SNIA
    - SyncIntegrationClients
    - Volatile

As you can see from this, there are more entries in the 32-bit section – the Wow6432Node - then there are in the 64-bit section.

We will talk more about this a few chapters down. Right now, I want to cover the Microsoft.Win32 namespace.

For each of the hives there is a similar registry name:

HKEY_CLASSES_ROOT

Registry.classesroot

HKEY_CURRENT_CONFIG

Registry.currentconfig

HKEY_CURRENT_USER

Registry.currentuser

HKEY_LOCAL_MACHINE

Registry.localmachine

HKEY_USERS

Registry.users

Also, assuming you are on a 64-bit operating system and you are compiling your program in x64 mode, you can open a hive using the below coding conventions.

```
        RegistryKey.OpenBaseKey(RegistryHive.ClassesRoot,
RegistryView.Default)
        RegistryKey.OpenBaseKey(RegistryHive.ClassesRoot,
RegistryView.Registry32)
        RegistryKey.OpenBaseKey(RegistryHive.ClassesRoot,
RegistryView.Registry64)
```

Same thing goes when you want to go to a remote machine

```
        RegistryKey.OpenRemoteBaseKey(RegistryHive.ClassesRoot,
ComputerName, RegistryView.Default)
        RegistryKey.OpenRemoteBaseKey(RegistryHive.ClassesRoot,
ComputerName, RegistryView.Registry32)
        RegistryKey.OpenRemoteBaseKey(RegistryHive.ClassesRoot,
ComputerName, RegistryView.Registry64)
```

There other thing I want to cover here – because I didn't elsewhere are the various datatypes. These are:

REG_SZ

REG_EXPANDED_SZ

REG_MULTI_SZ

REG_BINARY

REG_DWORD

REG_QWORD

Below, is how we deal with them:

```
Case RegistryValueKind.String

    newkind = "REG_SZ"

    newval = v.ToString()


Case RegistryValueKind.ExpandString

    newkind = "REG_EXPAND_SZ"

    newval = v.ToString()

Case RegistryValueKind.MultiString

    newkind = "REG_MULTI_SZ"

    newval = Join(v, ",")


Case RegistryValueKind.DWord

    newkind = "REG_DWORD"

    Dim c As String = Convert.ToString(v, 16)
    c = "0x" & c.PadLeft(8, "0")
```

```vbnet
Case RegistryValueKind.QWord

    newkind = "REG_QWORD"

    Dim l As Long = CType(v, Long)
    newval = "(0x" & Hex(l) & ") " & l.ToString()

Case RegistryValueKind.Binary

    newval = ""
    Dim tempstr As String = ""
    newkind = "REG_BINARY"
    For i As Integer = 0 To UBound(v)
        tempstr = Hex(v(i))
        If Len(tempstr) = 1 Then
            tempstr = "0" & tempstr
        End If
        newval = newval & tempstr & " "
        tempstr = ""
    Next
```

BASIC REGISTRY CODING
USING VB.NET
Keeping it simple

Okay so at this point you know something about the registry, it is time to focus on how to program it. With that said, let's start with a new VB.Net project and open Form1's code pane.

```
Public Class Form1

    Private Sub Form1_Load(sender As System.Object, e As
System.EventArgs) Handles MyBase.Load

    End Sub
End Class
```

Above the Public Class Form1, add Imports Microsoft.Win32 so that your code looks just like the view below:

```
Imports Microsoft.Win32
Public Class Form1

    Private Sub Form1_Load(sender As System.Object, e As
System.EventArgs) Handles MyBase.Load

    End Sub
End Class
```

Now you need to figure out what you want to do – what is the purpose for writing the code. In this example, I want to be able to know when a pending file rename operation is pending on my machine. That way I know when to close the programs I'm working on and restart my computer.

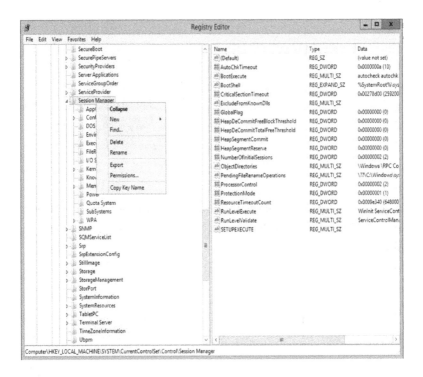

When I go to where I need to go in the registry, I right click on Session Manager and click the Copy Key Name. That returns:

HKEY_LOCAL_MACHINE\SYSTEM\CurrentControlSet\Control\Session Manager.

```
Dim regkey As RegistryKey =
Registry.LocalMachine.OpenSubKey("System\CurrentControlSet\Contro
l\Session Manager")
```

This will get us to the same place where we want to go as we did using regedit.

We can't assume that the Value Name will exist, so writing the code like this could cause you an issue:

```
Dim regkey As RegistryKey =
Registry.LocalMachine.OpenSubKey("System\CurrentControlSet\Contro
l\Session Manager")


Dim Value() As String =
regkey.GetValue("PendingFileRenameOperations")

For Each Va As String In Value
    Debug.Print(Va)
Next
```

Instead, what is a much better approach is to enumerate through the Value Names and then if it exists, if you want to know what the values are use the array of values logic to view the values.

But now, I want to get notified when one of these events happen:

```
Imports Microsoft.Win32
Public Class Form1

    Private Sub Form1_Load(sender As System.Object, e As
System.EventArgs) Handles MyBase.Load

        Me.Width = 900

        Dim str As String =
"System\CurrentControlSet\Control\Session Manager"

        Dim regkey As RegistryKey =
Registry.LocalMachine.OpenSubKey(str)

        Dim Names() As String = regkey.GetValueNames
        For Each n As String In Names

            If n = "PendingFileRenameOperations" Then
                Write_The_Report(regkey)
            End If

        Next
```

```vb
        End Sub

    Public Sub Write_The_Report(ByVal regkey As RegistryKey)

        Dim fso As Object =
CreateObject("Scripting.FileSystemObject")
        Dim txtstream As Object =
fso.OpenTextFile(System.Environment.CurrentDirectory &
"\Registry.html", 2, True, -2)
        txtstream.WriteLine("<hmtl>")
        txtstream.WriteLine("<head>")
        txtstream.WriteLine("<title></title>")
        txtstream.WriteLine("<style type='text/css'>")
        txtstream.WriteLine(".th")
        txtstream.WriteLine("{")
        txtstream.WriteLine("    BORDER-RIGHT: #999999 3px
solid;")
        txtstream.WriteLine("    PADDING-RIGHT: 6px;")
        txtstream.WriteLine("    PADDING-LEFT: 6px;")
        txtstream.WriteLine("    FONT-WEIGHT: Normal;")
        txtstream.WriteLine("    PADDING-BOTTOM: 6px;")
        txtstream.WriteLine("    COLOR: darkred;")
        txtstream.WriteLine("    LINE-HEIGHT: 14px;")
        txtstream.WriteLine("    PADDING-TOP: 6px;")
        txtstream.WriteLine("    BORDER-BOTTOM: #999 1px solid;")
        txtstream.WriteLine("    BACKGROUND-COLOR: #eeeeee;")
        txtstream.WriteLine("    FONT-FAMILY: font-family:
Cambria, serif;")
        txtstream.WriteLine("    FONT-SIZE: 12px;")
        txtstream.WriteLine("    text-align: left;")
        txtstream.WriteLine("    white-Space: nowrap;")
        txtstream.WriteLine("}")
        txtstream.WriteLine("td")
        txtstream.WriteLine("{")
        txtstream.WriteLine("    BORDER-RIGHT: #999999 3px
solid;")
        txtstream.WriteLine("    PADDING-RIGHT: 6px;")
        txtstream.WriteLine("    PADDING-LEFT: 6px;")
        txtstream.WriteLine("    FONT-WEIGHT: Normal;")
        txtstream.WriteLine("    PADDING-BOTTOM: 6px;")
        txtstream.WriteLine("    COLOR: navy;")
        txtstream.WriteLine("    LINE-HEIGHT: 14px;")
        txtstream.WriteLine("    PADDING-TOP: 6px;")
        txtstream.WriteLine("    BORDER-BOTTOM: #999 1px solid;")
        txtstream.WriteLine("    BACKGROUND-COLOR: #eeeeee;")
```

```vb
        txtstream.WriteLine("    FONT-FAMILY: font-family:
Cambria, serif;")
        txtstream.WriteLine("    FONT-SIZE: 12px;")
        txtstream.WriteLine("    text-align: left;")
        txtstream.WriteLine("    white-Space: nowrap;")
        txtstream.WriteLine("}")
        txtstream.WriteLine("</style>")
        txtstream.WriteLine("</head>")
        txtstream.WriteLine("<body bgColor=#252525>")
        txtstream.writeline("</br>")
        txtstream.writeline("</br>")
        txtstream.writeline("<center>")
        txtstream.writeline("<table Style=""Border:0;"">")
        txtstream.writeline("<tr><TH STYLE=""font-family:Calibri,
Sans-Serif;font-size:24px;color:white;"">Pending File Rename
Operation has been set</TH></tr>")
        txtstream.writeline("</table>")
        txtstream.writeline("</br>")
        txtstream.writeline("</br>")
        txtstream.writeline("<table style=border:Double;border-
width:1px;border-color:darkred;cellpadding=2 cellspacing=2
Width=0>")
        txtstream.writeline("<tr>")
        txtstream.writeline("    <th Class=th
align=""left"">Value Name</th>")
        txtstream.writeline("    <th Class=th align=""left"">Reg
Type</th>")
        txtstream.writeline("    <th Class=th
align=""left"">Value</th>")
        txtstream.writeline("</tr>")


        Dim regkind As String =
regkey.GetValueKind("PendingFileRenameOperations")
        Dim V() As String =
regkey.GetValue("PendingFileRenameOperations")
        Dim newkind As String = "REG_MULTI_SZ"
        Dim newval As String = ""
        For Each Va In V
            newval = newval & Va & "</br>"
        Next


        txtstream.writeline("<tr>")
        txtstream.writeline("    <td valign=""top""
align=""left"">PendingFileRenameOperations</td>")
```

```
        txtstream.writeline("      <td valign=""top""
align=""left"">" & newkind & "</td>")
        txtstream.writeline("      <td valign=""top""
align=""left"" Nowrap>" & newval & "</td>")
        txtstream.writeline("</tr>")
        txtstream.writeline("</table>")
        txtstream.writeline("</body>")
        txtstream.writeline("</html>")
        txtstream.Close()

        WebBrowser1.Navigate(System.Environment.CurrentDirectory
& "\Registry.html")

    End Sub
```

And that produces this:

Pending File Rename Operation has been set

Value Name	Reg Type	Value
PendingFileRenameOperations	REG_MULTI_SZ	\??\C:\Windows\system32\spool\V4Dirs\A883750E-11CC-4D48-A3B6-86E3714C53E2\94766af2.BUD
		\??\C:\Windows\system32\spool\V4Dirs\A883750E-11CC-4D48-A3B6-86E3714C53E2\94766af2.gpd
		\??\C:\Windows\system32\spool\V4Dirs\A883750E-11CC-4D48-A3B6-86E3714C53E2
		\??\C:\Windows\system32\spool\V4Dirs\511C59A8-F30E-4F42-868F-89C082F3892B\9a072afe.BUD
		\??\C:\Windows\system32\spool\V4Dirs\511C59A8-F30E-4F42-868F-89C082F3892B\9a072afe.gpd
		\??\C:\Windows\system32\spool\V4Dirs\511C59A8-F30E-4F42-868F-89C082F3892B
		\??\C:\Program Files\Mozilla Firefox\tobedeleted\moz3659.tmp
		\??\C:\Program Files\Mozilla Firefox\tobedeleted
		\??\C:\Program Files (x86)\Mozilla Maintenance Service\maintenanceservice_tmp.exe

One of the other problems I am faced with is knowing the details of my current TCPIP information. Simply put, I haven't a clue where it is located. So, naturally, I filtered for all the keys in HKEY_LOCAL_MACHINE\System\CurrentControlSet\Services for TCPIP.

```vb
Imports Microsoft.Win32
Public Class Form1

    Dim regkey As RegistryKey = Nothing
    Private Sub Form1_Load(sender As System.Object, e As
System.EventArgs) Handles MyBase.Load
        regkey = Registry.LocalMachine
        regkey.OpenSubKey("System\CurrentControlSet\Services\")
        Dim tn As TreeNode =
TreeView1.Nodes.Add("System\CurrentControlSet\Services\")
        tn.Tag = "System\CurrentControlSet\Services"
        Dim Names() As String =
regkey.OpenSubKey("System\CurrentControlSet\Services").GetSubKeyN
ames
        For Each n As String In Names
            Dim pos As Integer = InStr(LCase(n), "tcpip")
            If pos Then
                tn.Nodes.Add(n)
            End If
        Next

    End Sub

    Private Sub TreeView1_AfterSelect(sender As System.Object, e
As System.Windows.Forms.TreeViewEventArgs) Handles
TreeView1.AfterSelect

        If TreeView1.SelectedNode.Level = 0 Then Exit Sub

        Dim fp As String = TreeView1.SelectedNode.FullPath
        fp = Replace(fp, "\\", "\")
        If TreeView1.SelectedNode.Nodes.Count = 0 Then
            Dim Names() As String =
regkey.OpenSubKey(fp).GetSubKeyNames
            For Each N As String In Names
                TreeView1.SelectedNode.Nodes.Add(N)
            Next
        End If
        GetValues(fp)

    End Sub

    Public Sub GetValues(ByVal fullpath As String)
```

```vbnet
        Try
            If regkey.OpenSubKey(fullpath).GetValueNames.Count =
0 Then Exit Sub
        Catch ex As Exception
            Exit Sub
        End Try


        Dim vns() As String =
regkey.OpenSubKey(fullpath).GetValueNames


        Dim fso As Object =
CreateObject("Scripting.FileSystemObject")
        Dim txtstream As Object =
fso.OpenTextFile(System.Environment.CurrentDirectory &
"\Registry.html", 2, True, -2)
        txtstream.WriteLine("<hmtl>")
        txtstream.WriteLine("<head>")
        txtstream.WriteLine("<title></title>")
        txtstream.WriteLine("<style type='text/css'>")
        txtstream.WriteLine("th")
        txtstream.WriteLine("{")
        txtstream.WriteLine("      BORDER-RIGHT: #999999 3px
solid;")
        txtstream.WriteLine("      PADDING-RIGHT: 6px;")
        txtstream.WriteLine("      PADDING-LEFT: 6px;")
        txtstream.WriteLine("      FONT-WEIGHT: Normal;")
        txtstream.WriteLine("      PADDING-BOTTOM: 6px;")
        txtstream.WriteLine("      COLOR: darkred;")
        txtstream.WriteLine("      LINE-HEIGHT: 14px;")
        txtstream.WriteLine("      PADDING-TOP: 6px;")
        txtstream.WriteLine("      BORDER-BOTTOM: #999 1px solid;")
        txtstream.WriteLine("      BACKGROUND-COLOR: #eeeeee;")
        txtstream.WriteLine("      FONT-FAMILY: font-family:
Cambria, serif;")
        txtstream.WriteLine("      FONT-SIZE: 12px;")
        txtstream.WriteLine("      text-align: left;")
        txtstream.WriteLine("      white-Space: nowrap;")
        txtstream.WriteLine("}")
        txtstream.WriteLine("td")
        txtstream.WriteLine("{")
```

```
        txtstream.WriteLine("    BORDER-RIGHT: #999999 3px
solid;")
        txtstream.WriteLine("    PADDING-RIGHT: 6px;")
        txtstream.WriteLine("    PADDING-LEFT: 6px;")
        txtstream.WriteLine("    FONT-WEIGHT: Normal;")
        txtstream.WriteLine("    PADDING-BOTTOM: 6px;")
        txtstream.WriteLine("    COLOR: navy;")
        txtstream.WriteLine("    LINE-HEIGHT: 14px;")
        txtstream.WriteLine("    PADDING-TOP: 6px;")
        txtstream.WriteLine("    BORDER-BOTTOM: #999 1px solid;")
        txtstream.WriteLine("    BACKGROUND-COLOR: #eeeeee;")
        txtstream.WriteLine("    FONT-FAMILY: font-family:
Cambria, serif;")
        txtstream.WriteLine("    FONT-SIZE: 12px;")
        txtstream.WriteLine("    text-align: left;")
        txtstream.WriteLine("}")
        txtstream.WriteLine("input")
        txtstream.WriteLine("{")
        txtstream.WriteLine("    BORDER-RIGHT: #999999 3px
solid;")
        txtstream.WriteLine("    PADDING-RIGHT: 3px;")
        txtstream.WriteLine("    PADDING-LEFT: 3px;")
        txtstream.WriteLine("    FONT-WEIGHT: Bold;")
        txtstream.WriteLine("    PADDING-BOTTOM: 3px;")
        txtstream.WriteLine("    COLOR: white;")
        txtstream.WriteLine("    PADDING-TOP: 3px;")
        txtstream.WriteLine("    BORDER-BOTTOM: #999 1px solid;")
        txtstream.WriteLine("    BACKGROUND-COLOR: navy;")
        txtstream.WriteLine("    FONT-FAMILY: font-family:
Cambria, serif;")
        txtstream.WriteLine("    FONT-SIZE: 12px;")
        txtstream.WriteLine("    text-align: left;")
        'txtstream.WriteLine("    display: table-cell;")
        'txtstream.WriteLine("    white-Space: nowrap;")
        txtstream.WriteLine("    width: 100%;")
        txtstream.WriteLine("}")

        txtstream.WriteLine("</style>")
        txtstream.WriteLine("</head>")
        txtstream.WriteLine("<body bgColor=#252525>")
        txtstream.writeline("</br>")
        txtstream.writeline("</br>")
        txtstream.writeline("<center>")
        txtstream.writeline("</br>")
        txtstream.writeline("</br>")
```

```vbnet
        txtstream.writeline("<table style=border:Double;border-
width:1px;border-color:darkred;cellpadding=2 cellspacing=2
Width=0>")
        txtstream.writeline("<tr>")
        txtstream.writeline("    <th Class=th
align=""left"">Value Name</th>")
        txtstream.writeline("    <th Class=th align=""left"">Reg
Type</th>")
        txtstream.writeline("    <th Class=th
align=""left"">Value</th>")
        txtstream.writeline("</tr>")


        Dim newkind As String = ""
        Dim newval As String
        Dim v As Object

        Dim regkind As Object

        For Each vn As String In vns


            Try
                regkey.OpenSubKey(fullpath).GetValueKind(vn)
            Catch
                GoTo parrot
            End Try


            regkind =
regkey.OpenSubKey(fullpath).GetValueKind(vn)
            v = regkey.OpenSubKey(fullpath).GetValue(vn)

            newval = ""

            Select Case regkind


                Case RegistryValueKind.String

                    newkind = "REG_SZ"
                    newval = v.ToString()
```

```vbnet
        Case RegistryValueKind.ExpandString

            newkind = "REG_EXPAND_SZ"
            newval = v.ToString()

        Case RegistryValueKind.MultiString

            newkind = "REG_MULTI_SZ"
            newval = Join(v, ",")


        Case RegistryValueKind.DWord

            newkind = "REG_DWORD"

            Dim c As String = Convert.ToString(v, 16)
            c = "0x" & c.PadLeft(8, "0")

        Case RegistryValueKind.QWord

            newkind = "REG_QWORD"

            Dim l As Long = CType(v, Long)
            newval = "(0x" & Hex(l) & ") " & l.ToString()

        Case RegistryValueKind.Binary
            newval = ""
            Dim tempstr As String = ""
            newkind = "REG_BINARY"
            For i As Integer = 0 To UBound(v)
                tempstr = Hex(v(i))
                If Len(tempstr) = 1 Then
                    tempstr = "0" & tempstr
                End If
                newval = newval & tempstr & " "
                tempstr = ""
            Next

        Case RegistryValueKind.Unknown


    End Select


    txtstream.writeline("<tr>")
```

```
        txtstream.writeline("    <td valign=""top""
align=""left"">" & vn & "</td>")
        txtstream.writeline("    <td valign=""top""
align=""left"">" & newkind & "</td>")
        txtstream.writeline("    <td valign=""top""
align=""left""><input type=text value='" & newval &
"'></input></td>")
        txtstream.writeline("</tr>")


Parrot:


    Next

    txtstream.writeline("</table>")
    txtstream.writeline("</body>")
    txtstream.writeline("</html>")
    txtstream.Close()

    WebBrowser1.Navigate(System.Environment.CurrentDirectory
& "\Registry.html")


    End Sub
```

And found what I was looking for here:

And when I clicked on it, this is partial view of what was returned:

Value Name	Reg Type	Value
UseZeroBroadcast	REG_DWORD	████████████
EnableDeadGWDetect	REG_DWORD	████████████
EnableDHCP	REG_DWORD	████████████
NameServer	REG_SZ	████████████
Domain	REG_SZ	████████████
RegistrationEnabled	REG_DWORD	████████████
RegisterAdapterName	REG_DWORD	████████████
DhcpIPAddress	REG_SZ	192.168.0.96
DhcpSubnetMask	REG_SZ	255.255.255.0
DhcpServer	REG_SZ	192.168.0.1
Lease	REG_DWORD	████████████
LeaseObtainedTime	REG_DWORD	████████████
T1	REG_DWORD	████████████
T2	REG_DWORD	████████████
LeaseTerminatesTime	REG_DWORD	████████████
AddressType	REG_DWORD	████████████
IsServerNapAware	REG_DWORD	████████████
DhcpConnForceBroadcastFlag	REG_DWORD	████████████
DhcpNameServer	REG_SZ	68.105.28.11 68.105.29.11 68.105.28.12
DhcpDefaultGateway	REG_MULTI_SZ	192.168.0.1
DhcpSubnetMaskOpt	REG_MULTI_SZ	255.255.255.0
DhcpInterfaceOptions	REG_BINARY	FC 00 00 00 00 00 00 00 00 00 00 00 00 00 00 E1 C1 34 5
DhcpGatewayHardware	REG_BINARY	C0 A8 00 01 06 00 00 00 BE D1 65 A5 CE C3
DhcpGatewayHardwareCount	REG_DWORD	████████████

```vbnet
Imports Microsoft.Win32
Public Class Form1

    Dim regkey As RegistryKey = Nothing
    Private Sub Form1_Load(sender As System.Object, e As
System.EventArgs) Handles MyBase.Load


    End Sub

    Private Sub TreeView1_AfterSelect(sender As System.Object, e
As System.Windows.Forms.TreeViewEventArgs) Handles
TreeView1.AfterSelect

        Dim fp As String = ""

        If TreeView1.SelectedNode.Nodes.Count = 0 Then
            fp = TreeView1.SelectedNode.FullPath
            Dim Names() As String =
regkey.OpenSubKey(fp).GetSubKeyNames
            For Each N As String In Names
                TreeView1.SelectedNode.Nodes.Add(N)
            Next
        End If
        GetValues(fp)

    End Sub

    Public Sub GetValues(ByVal fullpath As String)


        Try
            If regkey.OpenSubKey(fullpath).GetValueNames.Count =
0 Then Exit Sub
        Catch ex As Exception
            Exit Sub
        End Try

        ListView1.Items.Clear()

        Dim vns() As String =
regkey.OpenSubKey(fullpath).GetValueNames
```

```vbnet
        Dim newkind As String = ""
        Dim newval As String
        Dim v As Object

        Dim regkind As Object

        For Each vn As String In vns


            Try
                regkey.OpenSubKey(fullpath).GetValueKind(vn)
            Catch
                GoTo parrot
            End Try


            regkind =
regkey.OpenSubKey(fullpath).GetValueKind(vn)
            v = regkey.OpenSubKey(fullpath).GetValue(vn)

            newval = ""

            Select Case regkind


                Case RegistryValueKind.String

                    newkind = "REG_SZ"
                    newval = v.ToString()


                Case RegistryValueKind.ExpandString

                    newkind = "REG_EXPAND_SZ"
                    newval = v.ToString()

                Case RegistryValueKind.MultiString

                    newkind = "REG_MULTI_SZ"
                    newval = Join(v, ",")


                Case RegistryValueKind.DWord
```

```vbnet
            newkind = "REG_DWORD"

            Dim c As String = Convert.ToString(v, 16)
            c = "0x" & c.PadLeft(8, "0")

        Case RegistryValueKind.QWord

            newkind = "REG_QWORD"

            Dim l As Long = CType(v, Long)
            newval = "(0x" & Hex(l) & ") " & l.ToString()

        Case RegistryValueKind.Binary
            newval = ""
            Dim tempstr As String = ""
            newkind = "REG_BINARY"
            For i As Integer = 0 To UBound(v)
                tempstr = Hex(v(i))
                If Len(tempstr) = 1 Then
                    tempstr = "0" & tempstr
                End If
                newval = newval & tempstr & " "
                tempstr = ""
            Next

        Case RegistryValueKind.Unknown


    End Select


    Dim li As ListViewItem = ListView1.Items.Add(vn)
    li.SubItems.Add(newkind)
    li.SubItems.Add(newval)



Parrot:


    Next
```

```vb
    End Sub

    Private Sub ComboBox1_SelectedIndexChanged(sender As
System.Object, e As System.EventArgs) Handles
ComboBox1.SelectedIndexChanged

        If ComboBox1.Text = "*Select A Hive*" Then Exit Sub

        Select Case ComboBox1.Text

            Case "HKEY_CLASSES_ROOT"

                regkey = Registry.ClassesRoot


            Case "HKEY_CURRENT_CONFIG"

                regkey = Registry.CurrentConfig

            Case "HKEY_CURRENT_USER"

                regkey = Registry.CurrentUser

            Case "HKEY_LOCAL_MACHINE"

                regkey = Registry.LocalMachine

            Case "HKEY_USERS"

                regkey = Registry.Users

        End Select

        TreeView1.Nodes.Clear()

        Dim names() As String = regkey.GetSubKeyNames

        For Each n As String In names

            TreeView1.Nodes.Add(n)

        Next
```

```
        End Sub
End Class
```

64-bit verses 32-bit
A horse of a different color

Up until now, I have been using the 32-bit version of the registry simply because I hadn't switched the OS CPU from x86 to x64. And, normally, if I hadn't already used the Configuration Manager to do so, x64 wouldn't be an option as shown below.

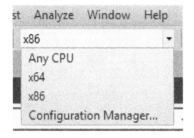

Once I've clicked on the Configuration Manager, I get this:

Again, normally, I wouldn't have x64 if I hadn't already changed it.

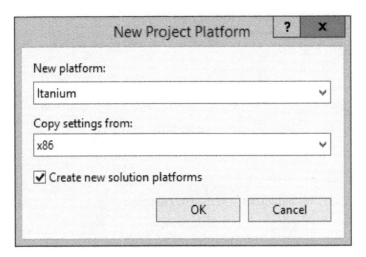

Same thing here. The additional x-64 would be a selection in the New Platform Combobox.

So, we cancel here and select the x64 option.

Why can't you just create another new project platform?

Because the program builds that project platform for you. And once it is done, you now have both 64-bit and 32-bit executables.

Here's the 32 bit:

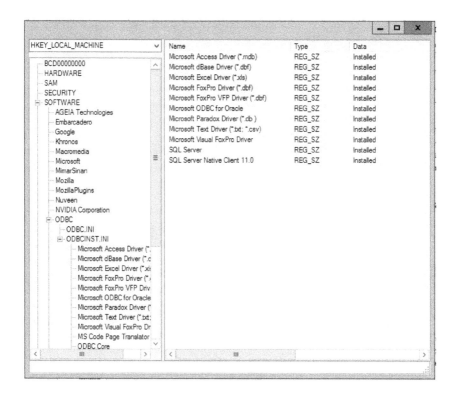

And here's the 64-bit:

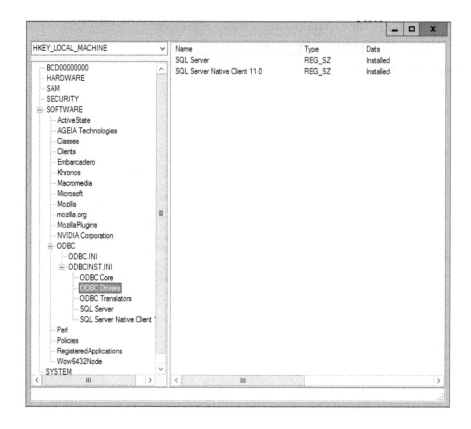

So, now, you have two registry viewers for the effort of programming up the first one.

Going for specific solutions

When I was working for Microsoft as the DCOM specialist, the one thing that I wanted to be able to do is select a class, then view the CLSID and APID Settings without having to memorize the classID.

```vbnet
Imports Microsoft.Win32

Public Class Form1

    Dim regkey1 As RegistryKey

    Private Sub Form1_Load(sender As System.Object, e As
System.EventArgs) Handles MyBase.Load

        Dim names() As String =
Registry.ClassesRoot.OpenSubKey("CLSID").GetSubKeyNames
        For Each n As String In names
            Dim regkey As RegistryKey =
Registry.ClassesRoot.OpenSubKey("CLSID\" & n & "\ProgID")
            If IsNothing(regkey) = False Then
                Try
                    Dim Value As String =
Registry.ClassesRoot.OpenSubKey("CLSID\" & n).GetValue("AppID")
                    If IsNothing(Value) = False Then
                        ComboBox1.Items.Add(regkey.GetValue(""))
                    End If
                Catch ex As Exception
                    Err.Clear()
                End Try
```

```vbnet
            End If

        Next

        Debug.Print(ComboBox1.Items.Count - 1)
        For x As Integer = 0 To ComboBox1.Items.Count - 1
            TreeView1.Nodes.Add(ComboBox1.Items(x))
        Next

    End Sub

    Private Sub TreeView1_AfterSelect(sender As System.Object, e
As System.Windows.Forms.TreeViewEventArgs) Handles
TreeView1.AfterSelect
        Try
            Dim Value As String =
Registry.ClassesRoot.OpenSubKey(TreeView1.SelectedNode.Text &
"\CLSID").GetValue("")
            Dim names() As String =
Registry.ClassesRoot.OpenSubKey("CLSID\" & Value).GetSubKeyNames
            ComboBox1.Items.Clear()
            TreeView2.Nodes.Clear()
            Dim tn As TreeNode = TreeView2.Nodes.Add(Value)
            For Each n As String In names
                tn.Nodes.Add(n)
            Next
        Catch ex As Exception

        End Try

    End Sub

    Private Sub TreeView2_AfterSelect(sender As System.Object, e
As System.Windows.Forms.TreeViewEventArgs) Handles
TreeView2.AfterSelect

        Dim fp As String = ""

        regkey1 = Registry.ClassesRoot.OpenSubKey("clsid\" &
TreeView2.SelectedNode.FullPath)

        If TreeView2.SelectedNode.Nodes.Count = 0 Then
            fp = TreeView2.SelectedNode.FullPath
            Dim Names() As String = regkey1.GetSubKeyNames
            For Each N As String In Names
```

```vb
            TreeView2.SelectedNode.Nodes.Add(N)
        Next
    End If

    GetValues()


End Sub

Public Sub GetValues()



    ListView1.Items.Clear()
    ListView2.Items.Clear()
    TreeView3.Nodes.Clear()

    Dim vns() As String = regkey1.GetValueNames()

    Dim newkind As String = ""
    Dim newval As String
    Dim v As Object

    Dim regkind As Object

    For Each vn As String In vns

        If LCase(vn) = "appid" Then
            DoAppID()
        End If

        Try
            regkey1.GetValueKind(vn)
        Catch
            GoTo parrot
        End Try


        regkind = regkey1.GetValueKind(vn)
        v = regkey1.GetValue(vn)

        newval = ""

        Select Case regkind
```

```vb
Case RegistryValueKind.String

    newkind = "REG_SZ"
    newval = v.ToString()


Case RegistryValueKind.ExpandString

    newkind = "REG_EXPAND_SZ"
    newval = v.ToString()

Case RegistryValueKind.MultiString

    newkind = "REG_MULTI_SZ"
    newval = Join(v, ",")


Case RegistryValueKind.DWord

    newkind = "REG_DWORD"

    Dim c As String = Convert.ToString(v, 16)
    c = "0x" & c.PadLeft(8, "0")

Case RegistryValueKind.QWord

    newkind = "REG_QWORD"

    Dim l As Long = CType(v, Long)
    newval = "(0x" & Hex(l) & ") " & l.ToString()

Case RegistryValueKind.Binary
    newval = ""
    Dim tempstr As String = ""
    newkind = "REG_BINARY"
    For i As Integer = 0 To UBound(v)
        tempstr = Hex(v(i))
        If Len(tempstr) = 1 Then
            tempstr = "0" & tempstr
        End If
        newval = newval & tempstr & " "
        tempstr = ""
    Next
```

```vbnet
            Case RegistryValueKind.Unknown


        End Select


        Dim li As ListViewItem = ListView2.Items.Add(vn)
        li.SubItems.Add(newkind)
        li.SubItems.Add(newval)



Parrot:


      Next



    End Sub

    Public Sub DoAppID()

        Dim newkind As String = ""
        Dim newval As String
        Dim v As Object


        Dim Value As String = regkey1.GetValue("AppID")

        TreeView3.Nodes.Add(Value)

        Try
            Dim regk As RegistryKey =
Registry.ClassesRoot.OpenSubKey("AppID\" & Value)
            Dim vNames() As String = regk.GetValueNames()


            Dim regkind As Object

            For Each vn As String In vNames

                Try
                    regk.GetValueKind(vn)
```

```
Catch
    GoTo kit
End Try


regkind = regk.GetValueKind(vn)
v = regk.GetValue(vn)

newval = ""

Select Case regkind


    Case RegistryValueKind.String

        newkind = "REG_SZ"
        newval = v.ToString()


    Case RegistryValueKind.ExpandString

        newkind = "REG_EXPAND_SZ"
        newval = v.ToString()

    Case RegistryValueKind.MultiString

        newkind = "REG_MULTI_SZ"
        newval = Join(v, ",")


    Case RegistryValueKind.DWord

        newkind = "REG_DWORD"

        Dim c As String = Convert.ToString(v, 16)
        c = "0x" & c.PadLeft(8, "0")

        newval = c

    Case RegistryValueKind.QWord

        newkind = "REG_QWORD"

        Dim l As Long = CType(v, Long)
```

```vbnet
                        newval = "(0x" & Hex(1) & ") " &
1.ToString()

                Case RegistryValueKind.Binary
                    newval = ""
                    Dim tempstr As String = ""
                    newkind = "REG_BINARY"
                    For i As Integer = 0 To UBound(v)
                        tempstr = Hex(v(i))
                        If Len(tempstr) = 1 Then
                            tempstr = "0" & tempstr
                        End If
                        newval = newval & tempstr & " "
                        tempstr = ""
                    Next

                Case RegistryValueKind.Unknown


            End Select


            Dim li As ListViewItem = ListView1.Items.Add(vn)
            li.SubItems.Add(newkind)
            li.SubItems.Add(newval)

kit:

            Next
        Catch ex As Exception

        End Try

    End Sub


End Class

The Visual:
```

Since I'm on a role here, What If I only wanted to look at Objects instead of both objects and controls?

```
Imports Microsoft.Win32
Public Class Form1
    Dim regkey1 As RegistryKey
    Private Sub Form1_Load(sender As System.Object, e As
System.EventArgs) Handles MyBase.Load
        Dim Names() As String =
Registry.ClassesRoot.OpenSubKey("clsid").GetSubKeyNames
        For Each n As String In Names
            If Mid(n, 1, 1) = "{" Then
```

```vbnet
            Dim regkey As RegistryKey =
Registry.ClassesRoot.OpenSubKey("clsid\" & n & "\Control")
            If IsNothing(regkey) = False Then

                regkey =
Registry.ClassesRoot.OpenSubKey("clsid\" & n & "\ProgID")
                If IsNothing(regkey) = False Then
                    Dim Value As String = regkey.GetValue("")
                    ComboBox1.Items.Add(Value)
                End If
            End If
        End If
    Next

    For x As Integer = 0 To ComboBox1.Items.Count - 1
        TreeView1.Nodes.Add(ComboBox1.Items(x))
    Next

End Sub

Private Sub TreeView1_AfterSelect(sender As System.Object, e
As System.Windows.Forms.TreeViewEventArgs) Handles
TreeView1.AfterSelect

    TreeView2.Nodes.Clear()
    ComboBox1.Items.Clear()

    Dim Value As String =
Registry.ClassesRoot.OpenSubKey(TreeView1.SelectedNode.Text &
"\CLSID").GetValue("")
    Dim tn As TreeNode = TreeView2.Nodes.Add(Value)
    Dim regkey As RegistryKey =
Registry.ClassesRoot.OpenSubKey("clsid\" & Value)
    Dim Names() As String = regkey.GetSubKeyNames
    For Each n As String In Names
        ComboBox1.Items.Add(n)
    Next

    For x As Integer = 0 To ComboBox1.Items.Count - 1
        tn.Nodes.Add(ComboBox1.Items(x))
    Next

End Sub
```

```vbnet
    Private Sub TreeView2_AfterSelect(sender As System.Object, e
As System.Windows.Forms.TreeViewEventArgs) Handles
TreeView2.AfterSelect

        Dim fp As String = ""

        regkey1 = Registry.ClassesRoot.OpenSubKey("clsid\" &
TreeView2.SelectedNode.FullPath)

        If TreeView2.SelectedNode.Nodes.Count = 0 Then
            fp = TreeView2.SelectedNode.FullPath
            Dim Names() As String = regkey1.GetSubKeyNames
            For Each N As String In Names
                TreeView2.SelectedNode.Nodes.Add(N)
            Next
        End If

        GetValues()


    End Sub

    Public Sub GetValues()



        ListView1.Items.Clear()


        Dim vns() As String = regkey1.GetValueNames()

        Dim newkind As String = ""
        Dim newval As String
        Dim v As Object

        Dim regkind As Object

        For Each vn As String In vns


            Try
                regkey1.GetValueKind(vn)
            Catch
                GoTo parrot
            End Try
```

```vbnet
regkind = regkey1.GetValueKind(vn)
v = regkey1.GetValue(vn)

newval = ""

Select Case regkind

    Case RegistryValueKind.String

        newkind = "REG_SZ"
        newval = v.ToString()


    Case RegistryValueKind.ExpandString

        newkind = "REG_EXPAND_SZ"
        newval = v.ToString()

    Case RegistryValueKind.MultiString

        newkind = "REG_MULTI_SZ"
        newval = Join(v, ",")


    Case RegistryValueKind.DWord

        newkind = "REG_DWORD"

        Dim c As String = Convert.ToString(v, 16)
        c = "0x" & c.PadLeft(8, "0")

    Case RegistryValueKind.QWord

        newkind = "REG_QWORD"

        Dim l As Long = CType(v, Long)
        newval = "(0x" & Hex(l) & ") " & l.ToString()

    Case RegistryValueKind.Binary
        newval = ""
        Dim tempstr As String = ""
        newkind = "REG_BINARY"
```

```
            For i As Integer = 0 To UBound(v)
                tempstr = Hex(v(i))
                If Len(tempstr) = 1 Then
                    tempstr = "0" & tempstr
                End If
                newval = newval & tempstr & " "
                tempstr = ""
            Next

        Case RegistryValueKind.Unknown


    End Select


    Dim li As ListViewItem = ListView1.Items.Add(vn)
    li.SubItems.Add(newkind)
    li.SubItems.Add(newval)
```

Parrot:

```
        Next


    End Sub

End Class
```

And the IDE View:

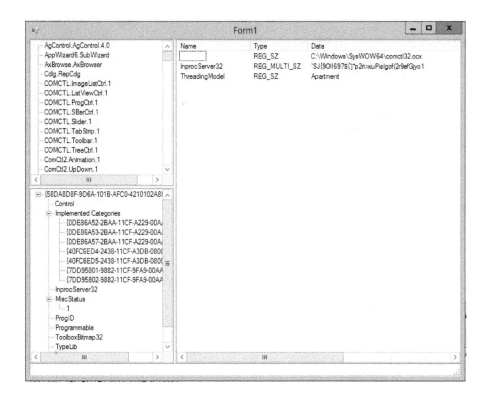

To create one of these for just objects, switch the form load code to this:

```
    Private Sub Form1_Load(sender As System.Object, e As
System.EventArgs) Handles MyBase.Load
        Dim Names() As String =
Registry.ClassesRoot.OpenSubKey("clsid").GetSubKeyNames
        For Each n As String In Names
            If Mid(n, 1, 1) = "{" Then
                Dim regkey As RegistryKey =
Registry.ClassesRoot.OpenSubKey("clsid\" & n & "\Control")
                If IsNothing(regkey) = True Then
                    regkey =
Registry.ClassesRoot.OpenSubKey("clsid\" & n & "\ProgID")
                If IsNothing(regkey) = False Then
                    Dim Value As String = regkey.GetValue("")
                    If IsNothing(Value) = False Then
                        ComboBox1.Items.Add(Value)
```

```
                    End If
                End If
            End If
        End If
    Next

    For x As Integer = 0 To ComboBox1.Items.Count - 1
        TreeView1.Nodes.Add(ComboBox1.Items(x))
    Next

End Sub
```

You will see:

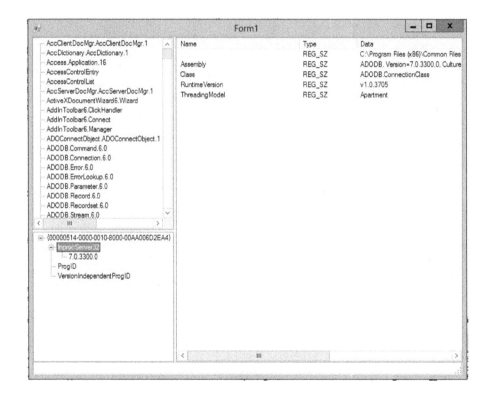

Data specific registry viewers

Essentially, there are three data specific views that many of us programmers should be focused on with respect to 32-bit:

What Providers are installed that are 32-bit
What ODBC Drivers are installed that are 32-bit
What ISAMs are installed that are 32-bit

And with 64-bit:

What Providers are installed that are 64-bit
What ODBC Drivers are installed that are 64-bit
What ISAMs are installed that are 64-bit

In the case of 64-bit, we know we can find the ODBC Drivers here:
HKEY_LOCAL_MACHINE\SOFTWARE\ODBC\ODBCINST.INI\ODBC Drivers
In the case of 64-bit providers, we're going here:
HKEY_LOCAL_MACHINE\SOFTWARE\Classes

In the case of installed 32-bit, we know we can find the ODBC drivers here:
HKEY_LOCAL_MACHINE\SOFTWARE\Wow6432Node\ODBC\ODBCINST.INI
In the case of installed 32-bit providers, we can go here:
HKEY_LOCAL_MACHINE\SOFTWARE\Wow6432Node\Classes
In the case of installed ISAMs, we can go here:
HKEY_LOCAL_MACHINE\SOFTWARE\Wow6432Node\Microsoft\Jet

So, here's the code for the 32-bit ISAM discovery:

```vb
Imports Microsoft.Win32
Public Class Form3

    Private Sub TreeView1_AfterSelect(ByVal sender As
System.Object, ByVal e As System.Windows.Forms.TreeViewEventArgs)
Handles TreeView1.AfterSelect
        Dim fso As Object =
CreateObject("Scripting.FileSystemObject")
        Dim txtstream As Object =
fso.OpenTextFile(Application.StartupPath & "\" &
Replace(TreeView1.SelectedNode.Text, ".", "_") & ".html", 2,
True, -2)
        txtstream.writeline("<hmtl>")
        txtstream.writeline("<head>")
        txtstream.writeline("<title></title>")
        txtstream.writeline("<style type=""text/css"">")
        txtstream.writeline(".myclass")
        txtstream.writeline("{")
        txtstream.writeline("    BORDER-RIGHT: #999999 3px
solid;")
        txtstream.writeline("    PADDING-RIGHT: 6px;")
        txtstream.writeline("    PADDING-LEFT: 6px;")
        txtstream.writeline("    PADDING-BOTTOM: 6px;")
        txtstream.writeline("    LINE-HEIGHT: 14px;")
        txtstream.writeline("    PADDING-TOP: 6px;")
        txtstream.writeline("    BORDER-BOTTOM: #999 1px solid;")
        txtstream.writeline("    BACKGROUND-COLOR: #eeeeee;")
        txtstream.writeline("
filter:progid:DXImageTransform.Microsoft.Shadow(color='silver',
Direction=135, Strength=16)")
        txtstream.writeline("}")
        txtstream.writeline(".myclass1")
        txtstream.writeline("{")
        txtstream.writeline("    BORDER-RIGHT: #999999 1px
solid;")
        txtstream.writeline("    PADDING-RIGHT: 2px;")
        txtstream.writeline("    PADDING-LEFT: 6px;")
        txtstream.writeline("    PADDING-BOTTOM: 2px;")
        txtstream.writeline("    LINE-HEIGHT: 20px;")
        txtstream.writeline("    PADDING-TBOTTOMOP: 3px;")
        txtstream.writeline("    BORDER-: #999 1px solid;")
```

```
        txtstream.writeline("    BACKGROUND-COLOR: #FFFFFF;")
        txtstream.writeline("
filter:progid:DXImageTransform.Microsoft.Shadow(color='black',
Direction=135, Strength=2)")
        txtstream.writeline("}")
        txtstream.writeline(".myclass2")
        txtstream.writeline("{")
        txtstream.writeline("BORDER-RIGHT: #999999 3px solid;")
        txtstream.writeline("BORDER-LEFT: #999999 3px solid;")
        txtstream.writeline("BORDER-TOP: #999999 3px solid;")
        txtstream.writeline("BORDER-BOTTOM: #999999 3px solid;")
        txtstream.writeline("PADDING-RIGHT: 1px;")
        txtstream.writeline("PADDING-LEFT: 1px;")
        txtstream.writeline("PADDING-BOTTOM: 1px;")
        txtstream.writeline("LINE-HEIGHT: 30px;")
        txtstream.writeline("PADDING-TOP: 1px;")
        txtstream.writeline("BACKGROUND-COLOR: navy;")
        txtstream.writeline("COLOR: AntiqueDarkRed;")
        txtstream.writeline("}")
        txtstream.writeline(".myclass3")
        txtstream.writeline("{")
        txtstream.writeline("BORDER-RIGHT: #666666 1px groove;")
        txtstream.writeline("BORDER-LEFT: #999999 1px groove;")
        txtstream.writeline("BORDER-TOP: AntiqueDarkRed 1px
groove;")
        txtstream.writeline("BORDER-BOTTOM: #000000 1px groove;")
        txtstream.writeline("PADDING-RIGHT: 1px;")
        txtstream.writeline("PADDING-LEFT: 1px;")
        txtstream.writeline("PADDING-BOTTOM: 1px;")
        txtstream.writeline("LINE-HEIGHT: 1px;")
        txtstream.writeline("PADDING-TOP: 1px;")
        txtstream.writeline("COLOR: navy;")

txtstream.writeline("filter:progid:DXImageTransform.Microsoft.Sha
dow(color='silver', Direction=135, Strength=2)")
        txtstream.writeline("}")
        txtstream.writeline(".myclass4")
        txtstream.writeline("{")
        txtstream.writeline("COLOR: goldenrod;")

txtstream.writeline("filter:progid:DXImageTransform.Microsoft.Sha
dow(color='black', Direction=135, Strength=4)")
        txtstream.writeline("}")
        txtstream.writeline("a")
        txtstream.writeline("{")
```

```vb
        txtstream.writeline("font-size: 12px;")
        txtstream.writeline("color: navy;")
        txtstream.writeline("Font -family: Cambria , serif")
        txtstream.writeline("}")
        txtstream.writeline("</style>")
        txtstream.writeline("</head>")
        txtstream.writeline("<body style=""margin: 0px 15px""
text=""#000000"" vlink=""#a89e89"" alink=""#a89e89""
link=""#c8c1b5"" bgcolor=""#ffffff"" leftmargin=""0""
topmargin=""0"" marginwidth=""0"">")
        txtstream.writeline("<center>")
        txtstream.writeline("<br>")
        txtstream.writeline("<br>")
        txtstream.writeline("<table>")
        txtstream.writeline("<tr><TH Nowrap STYLE=""FONT-
WEIGHT:normal; FONT-SIZE: 24px; COLOR: navy; FONT-STYLE: normal;
FONT-FAMILY: Times New Roman"">Planet Management
Professionals  </TH></tr>")
        txtstream.writeline("<tr><TH Nowrap STYLE=""FONT-
WEIGHT:normal; FONT-SIZE: 48px; COLOR: navy; FONT-STYLE: normal;
FONT-FAMILY: Edwardian Script ITC"">System Management
Presentation Tools</TH></tr>")
        txtstream.writeline("<tr><TH Nowrap STYLE=""FONT-
WEIGHT:normal; FONT-SIZE: 12px; COLOR: DarkSlateGray; FONT-STYLE:
normal; FONT-FAMILY: font-family:Calibri, Sans-Serif"">" &
DateTime.Now & "</TH></tr>")
        txtstream.writeline("</table>")
        txtstream.writeline("</center>")
        txtstream.writeline("<br>")
        txtstream.writeline("<table cellpadding=1 cellspacing=1
width=100%>")
        txtstream.writeline("<tr><TH Nowrap colspan=2
STYLE=""FONT-WEIGHT:normal; FONT-SIZE: 18px; COLOR: black; FONT-
STYLE: normal; font-family:Calibri, Sans-Serif;""><b><u>File
Information</u></b></TH></tr>")

        Dim objs As Object =
GetObject("winmgmts:\\.\root\cimv2").ExecQuery("Select * From
CIM_DataFile where name='" & Replace(TreeView1.SelectedNode.Tag,
"\", "\\") & "'")
        For Each obj As Object In objs
            For Each prop As Object In obj.Properties_
                txtstream.writeline("<tr>")
                txtstream.writeline("<th width=50% align=right
Nowrap STYLE=""FONT-WEIGHT:normal; FONT-SIZE: 12px; COLOR:
```

```vb
DarkRed; FONT-STYLE: normal; font-family:Times New Roman;"">" &
prop.Name & "</th>")
                txtstream.writeline("<td width=50% align=left
Nowrap STYLE=""FONT-WEIGHT:normal; FONT-SIZE: 12px; COLOR: navy;
FONT-STYLE: normal; font-family:Times New Roman;"">" & prop.Value
& "</td>")
                txtstream.writeline("</tr>")
            Next
            Exit For
        Next
        txtstream.writeline("</table>")
        txtstream.writeline("<br>")
        txtstream.writeline("<table cellpadding=1 cellspacing=1
width=100%>")
        txtstream.writeline("<tr><TH Nowrap colspan=2
STYLE=""FONT-WEIGHT:normal; FONT-SIZE: 18px; COLOR: black; FONT-
STYLE: normal; font-family:Calibri, Sans-Serif;""><b><u>File
Version Information</u></b></TH></tr>")
        Dim v As FileVersionInfo =
FileVersionInfo.GetVersionInfo(TreeView1.SelectedNode.Tag)
        For Each p As Object In v.GetType().GetProperties
            txtstream.writeline("<tr>")
            txtstream.writeline("<th width=50% align=right Nowrap
STYLE=""FONT-WEIGHT:normal; FONT-SIZE: 12px; COLOR: DarkRed;
FONT-STYLE: normal; font-family:Times New Roman;"">" & p.Name &
"</th>")
            Dim pv As Object = v.GetType().InvokeMember(p.Name,
Reflection.BindingFlags.GetProperty, Nothing, v, Nothing)
            txtstream.writeline("<td width=50% align=left Nowrap
STYLE=""FONT-WEIGHT:normal; FONT-SIZE: 12px; COLOR: navy; FONT-
STYLE: normal; font-family:Times New Roman;"">" & pv.ToString() &
"</td>")
            txtstream.writeline("</tr>")
        Next
        txtstream.writeline("</table>")
        txtstream.writeline("</body>")
        txtstream.writeline("</html>")
        txtstream.Close()
        txtstream = Nothing
        fso = Nothing

        WebBrowser1.Navigate(Application.StartupPath & "\" &
Replace(TreeView1.SelectedNode.Text, ".", "_") & ".html")
```

```vb
    End Sub

    Private Sub Form3_Load(sender As System.Object, e As
System.EventArgs) Handles MyBase.Load
        Dim names() As String

        Try
            names =
Registry.LocalMachine.OpenSubKey("Software\WOW6432NODE\Microsoft\
Jet\3.5\ISAM Formats").GetSubKeyNames()
            For x As Integer = 0 To names.GetLength(0) - 1
                Dim tn As TreeNode =
TreeView1.Nodes.Add(names.GetValue(x))
                Dim value As String =
Registry.LocalMachine.OpenSubKey("Software\WOW6432NODE\Microsoft\
Jet\3.5\ISAM Formats\" & names.GetValue(x)).GetValue("Engine")
                tn.Tag =
Replace(Registry.LocalMachine.OpenSubKey("Software\WOW6432NODE\Mi
crosoft\Jet\3.5\Engines\" & value).GetValue("Win32"), "System32",
"WOW6432Node")
            Next
        Catch ex As Exception

        End Try


        names =
Registry.LocalMachine.OpenSubKey("Software\WOW6432NODE\Microsoft\
Jet\4.0\ISAM Formats").GetSubKeyNames()
        For x As Integer = 0 To names.GetLength(0) - 1
            Dim tn As TreeNode =
TreeView2.Nodes.Add(names.GetValue(x))
            Dim value As String =
Registry.LocalMachine.OpenSubKey("Software\WOW6432NODE\Microsoft\
Jet\4.0\ISAM Formats\" & names.GetValue(x)).GetValue("Engine")
            tn.Tag =
Replace(Registry.LocalMachine.OpenSubKey("Software\WOW6432NODE\Mi
crosoft\Jet\4.0\Engines\" & value).GetValue("Win32"), "System32",
"WOW6432Node")
        Next
    End Sub

    Private Sub TreeView2_AfterSelect(sender As System.Object, e
As System.Windows.Forms.TreeViewEventArgs) Handles
TreeView2.AfterSelect
```

```vbnet
        Dim fso As Object =
CreateObject("Scripting.FileSystemObject")
        Dim txtstream As Object =
fso.OpenTextFile(Application.StartupPath & "\" &
Replace(TreeView2.SelectedNode.Text, ".", "_") & ".html", 2,
True, -2)
        txtstream.writeline("<hmtl>")
        txtstream.writeline("<head>")
        txtstream.writeline("<title></title>")
        txtstream.writeline("<style type=""text/css"">")
        txtstream.writeline(".myclass")
        txtstream.writeline("{")
        txtstream.writeline("    BORDER-RIGHT: #999999 3px
solid;")
        txtstream.writeline("    PADDING-RIGHT: 6px;")
        txtstream.writeline("    PADDING-LEFT: 6px;")
        txtstream.writeline("    PADDING-BOTTOM: 6px;")
        txtstream.writeline("    LINE-HEIGHT: 14px;")
        txtstream.writeline("    PADDING-TOP: 6px;")
        txtstream.writeline("    BORDER-BOTTOM: #999 1px solid;")
        txtstream.writeline("    BACKGROUND-COLOR: #eeeeee;")
        txtstream.writeline("
filter:progid:DXImageTransform.Microsoft.Shadow(color='silver',
Direction=135, Strength=16)")
        txtstream.writeline("}")
        txtstream.writeline(".myclass1")
        txtstream.writeline("{")
        txtstream.writeline("    BORDER-RIGHT: #999999 1px
solid;")
        txtstream.writeline("    PADDING-RIGHT: 2px;")
        txtstream.writeline("    PADDING-LEFT: 6px;")
        txtstream.writeline("    PADDING-BOTTOM: 2px;")
        txtstream.writeline("    LINE-HEIGHT: 20px;")
        txtstream.writeline("    PADDING-TBOTTOMOP: 3px;")
        txtstream.writeline("    BORDER-: #999 1px solid;")
        txtstream.writeline("    BACKGROUND-COLOR: #FFFFFF;")
        txtstream.writeline("
filter:progid:DXImageTransform.Microsoft.Shadow(color='black',
Direction=135, Strength=2)")
        txtstream.writeline("}")
        txtstream.writeline(".myclass2")
        txtstream.writeline("{")
        txtstream.writeline("BORDER-RIGHT: #999999 3px solid;")
        txtstream.writeline("BORDER-LEFT: #999999 3px solid;")
        txtstream.writeline("BORDER-TOP: #999999 3px solid;")
```

```
        txtstream.writeline("BORDER-BOTTOM: #999999 3px solid;")
        txtstream.writeline("PADDING-RIGHT: 1px;")
        txtstream.writeline("PADDING-LEFT: 1px;")
        txtstream.writeline("PADDING-BOTTOM: 1px;")
        txtstream.writeline("LINE-HEIGHT: 30px;")
        txtstream.writeline("PADDING-TOP: 1px;")
        txtstream.writeline("BACKGROUND-COLOR: navy;")
        txtstream.writeline("COLOR: AntiqueDarkRed;")
        txtstream.writeline("}")
        txtstream.writeline(".myclass3")
        txtstream.writeline("{")
        txtstream.writeline("BORDER-RIGHT: #666666 1px groove;")
        txtstream.writeline("BORDER-LEFT: #999999 1px groove;")
        txtstream.writeline("BORDER-TOP: AntiqueDarkRed 1px
groove;")
        txtstream.writeline("BORDER-BOTTOM: #000000 1px groove;")
        txtstream.writeline("PADDING-RIGHT: 1px;")
        txtstream.writeline("PADDING-LEFT: 1px;")
        txtstream.writeline("PADDING-BOTTOM: 1px;")
        txtstream.writeline("LINE-HEIGHT: 1px;")
        txtstream.writeline("PADDING-TOP: 1px;")
        txtstream.writeline("COLOR: navy;")

txtstream.writeline("filter:progid:DXImageTransform.Microsoft.Sha
dow(color='silver', Direction=135, Strength=2)")
        txtstream.writeline("}")
        txtstream.writeline(".myclass4")
        txtstream.writeline("{")
        txtstream.writeline("COLOR: goldenrod;")

txtstream.writeline("filter:progid:DXImageTransform.Microsoft.Sha
dow(color='black', Direction=135, Strength=4)")
        txtstream.writeline("}")
        txtstream.writeline("a")
        txtstream.writeline("{")
        txtstream.writeline("font-size: 12px;")
        txtstream.writeline("color: navy;")
        txtstream.writeline("Font -family: Cambria , serif")
        txtstream.writeline("}")
        txtstream.writeline("</style>")
        txtstream.writeline("</head>")
        txtstream.writeline("<body style=""margin: 0px 0px 15px""
text=""#000000"" vlink=""#a89e89"" alink=""#a89e89""
link=""#c8c1b5"" bgcolor=""#ffffff"" leftmargin=""0""
topmargin=""0"" marginwidth=""0"">")
```

```
        txtstream.writeline("<center>")
        txtstream.writeline("<br>")
        txtstream.writeline("<br>")
        txtstream.writeline("<table>")
        txtstream.writeline("<tr><TH Nowrap STYLE=""FONT-
WEIGHT:normal; FONT-SIZE: 24px; COLOR: navy; FONT-STYLE: normal;
FONT-FAMILY: Times New Roman"">Planet Management
Professionals  </TH></tr>")
        txtstream.writeline("<tr><TH Nowrap STYLE=""FONT-
WEIGHT:normal; FONT-SIZE: 48px; COLOR: navy; FONT-STYLE: normal;
FONT-FAMILY: Edwardian Script ITC"">System Management
Presentation Tools</TH></tr>")
        txtstream.writeline("<tr><TH Nowrap STYLE=""FONT-
WEIGHT:normal; FONT-SIZE: 12px; COLOR: DarkSlateGray; FONT-STYLE:
normal; FONT-FAMILY: font-family:Calibri, Sans-Serif"">" &
DateTime.Now & "</TH></tr>")
        txtstream.writeline("</table>")
        txtstream.writeline("</center>")
        txtstream.writeline("<br>")
        txtstream.writeline("<table cellpadding=1 cellspacing=1
width=100%>")
        txtstream.writeline("<tr><TH Nowrap colspan=2
STYLE=""FONT-WEIGHT:normal; FONT-SIZE: 18px; COLOR: black; FONT-
STYLE: normal; font-family:Calibri, Sans-Serif;""><b><u>File
Information</u></b></TH></tr>")

        Dim objs As Object =
GetObject("winmgmts:\\.\root\cimv2").ExecQuery("Select * From
CIM_DataFile where name='" & Replace(TreeView2.SelectedNode.Tag,
"\", "\\") & "'")
        For Each obj As Object In objs
            For Each prop As Object In obj.Properties_
                txtstream.writeline("<tr>")
                txtstream.writeline("<th width=50% align=right
Nowrap STYLE=""FONT-WEIGHT:normal; FONT-SIZE: 12px; COLOR:
DarkRed; FONT-STYLE: normal; font-family:Times New Roman;"">" &
prop.Name & "</th>")
                txtstream.writeline("<td width=50% align=left
Nowrap STYLE=""FONT-WEIGHT:normal; FONT-SIZE: 12px; COLOR: navy;
FONT-STYLE: normal; font-family:Times New Roman;"">" & prop.Value
& "</td>")
                txtstream.writeline("</tr>")
            Next
            Exit For
        Next
```

```
            txtstream.writeline("</table>")
            txtstream.writeline("<br>")
            txtstream.writeline("<table cellpadding=1 cellspacing=1
width=100%>")
            txtstream.writeline("<tr><TH Nowrap colspan=2
STYLE=""FONT-WEIGHT:normal; FONT-SIZE: 18px; COLOR: black; FONT-
STYLE: normal; font-family:Calibri, Sans-Serif;""><b><u>File
Version Information</u></b></TH></tr>")
            Dim v As FileVersionInfo =
FileVersionInfo.GetVersionInfo(TreeView2.SelectedNode.Tag)
            For Each p As Object In v.GetType().GetProperties
                txtstream.writeline("<tr>")
                txtstream.writeline("<th width=50% align=right Nowrap
STYLE=""FONT-WEIGHT:normal; FONT-SIZE: 12px; COLOR: DarkRed;
FONT-STYLE: normal; font-family:Times New Roman;"">" & p.Name &
"</th>")
                Dim pv As Object = v.GetType().InvokeMember(p.Name,
Reflection.BindingFlags.GetProperty, Nothing, v, Nothing)
                txtstream.writeline("<td width=50% align=left Nowrap
STYLE=""FONT-WEIGHT:normal; FONT-SIZE: 12px; COLOR: navy; FONT-
STYLE: normal; font-family:Times New Roman;"">" & pv.ToString() &
"</td>")
                txtstream.writeline("</tr>")
            Next
        txtstream.writeline("</table>")
        txtstream.writeline("</body>")
        txtstream.writeline("</html>")
        txtstream.Close()
        txtstream = Nothing
        fso = Nothing

        WebBrowser1.Navigate(Application.StartupPath & "\" &
Replace(TreeView2.SelectedNode.Text, ".", "_") & ".html")
    End Sub
```

And what the form looks like:

The Code for the Drivers:

```vbnet
Imports Microsoft.Win32

Public Class Form2
```

```vb
    Private Sub Form2_Load(sender As System.Object, e As
System.EventArgs) Handles MyBase.Load


        Dim fso As Object =
CreateObject("Scripting.FileSystemObject")
        Dim txtstream As Object =
fso.OpenTextFile(Application.StartupPath & "\Drivers.html", 2,
True, -2)
        txtstream.writeline("<hmtl>")
        txtstream.writeline("<head>")
        txtstream.writeline("<title></title>")
        txtstream.writeline("</head>")
        txtstream.writeline("<body style=""margin: 0px 0px 15px""
text=""#000000"" vlink=""#a89e89"" alink=""#a89e89""
link=""#c8c1b5"" bgcolor=""#ffffff"" leftmargin=""0""
topmargin=""0"" marginwidth=""0"">")
        txtstream.writeline("<center>")
        txtstream.writeline("<br>")
        txtstream.writeline("<br>")
        txtstream.writeline("<table>")
        txtstream.writeline("<tr><TH Nowrap STYLE=""FONT-
WEIGHT:normal; FONT-SIZE: 24px; COLOR: navy; FONT-STYLE: normal;
FONT-FAMILY: Times New Roman"">Windows Management
Experts  </TH></tr>")
        txtstream.writeline("<tr><TH Nowrap STYLE=""FONT-
WEIGHT:normal; FONT-SIZE: 48px; COLOR: navy; FONT-STYLE: normal;
FONT-FAMILY: Edwardian Script ITC"">System Management
Presentation Tools</TH></tr>")
        txtstream.writeline("<tr><TH Nowrap STYLE=""FONT-
WEIGHT:normal; FONT-SIZE: 12px; COLOR: DarkSlateGray; FONT-STYLE:
normal; FONT-FAMILY: font-family:Calibri, Sans-Serif"">" &
DateTime.Now & "</TH></tr>")
        txtstream.writeline("</table>")
        txtstream.writeline("</center>")
        txtstream.writeline("<br>")
        txtstream.writeline("<table cellpadding=1 cellspacing=1
width=100%>")


        Dim p As String = "Software\ODBC\ODBCINST.INI\ODBC
Drivers"
```

```vbnet
        txtstream.writeline("<tr><TH Nowrap colspan=2
STYLE=""FONT-WEIGHT:normal; FONT-SIZE: 18px; COLOR: black; FONT-
STYLE: normal; font-family:Calibri, Sans-Serif;""><b><u>" & p &
"</u></b></TH></tr>")


        Dim Names() As String =
Registry.LocalMachine.OpenSubKey(p).GetValueNames
        For x As Integer = 0 To Names.GetLength(0) - 1

            txtstream.writeline("<tr>")
            txtstream.writeline("<th width=50% align=right Nowrap
STYLE=""FONT-WEIGHT:normal; FONT-SIZE: 12px; COLOR: DarkRed;
FONT-STYLE: normal; font-family:Times New
Roman;"">Name: </th>")
            txtstream.writeline("<td width=50% align=left Nowrap
STYLE=""FONT-WEIGHT:normal; FONT-SIZE: 12px; COLOR: navy; FONT-
STYLE: normal; font-family:Times New Roman;"">" &
Names.GetValue(x) & "</td>")
            txtstream.writeline("</tr>")
        Next
        txtstream.writeline("<tr>")
        txtstream.writeline("</table>")
        txtstream.writeline("</th></tr>")
        txtstream.writeline("</table>")
        txtstream.writeline("</body>")
        txtstream.writeline("</html>")
        txtstream.Close()

        WebBrowser1.Navigate(Application.StartupPath &
"\Drivers.html")


    End Sub

    Public Sub Create_Report()


        Dim x As Integer = 0

        Dim DisplayName As String = ""
        Dim DisplayVersion As String = ""
        Dim HelpLink As String = ""
        Dim HelpTelephone As String = ""
        Dim InstallDate As String = ""
```

```vb
        Dim InstallLocation As String = ""
        Dim Publisher As String = ""
        Dim UninstallString As String = ""


        Dim Names() As String =
Registry.LocalMachine.OpenSubKey("SOFTWARE\Microsoft\Windows\Curr
entVersion\Uninstall").GetSubKeyNames
        For y As Integer = 0 To Names.GetLength(0) - 1
            If Mid(Names.GetValue(y), 1, 1) = "{" Then
                DisplayName =
Registry.LocalMachine.OpenSubKey("SOFTWARE\Microsoft\Windows\Curr
entVersion\Uninstall\" &
Names.GetValue(y)).GetValue("DisplayName")
                If DisplayName Is Nothing = True Then
                    DisplayName = ""
                End If
                DisplayVersion =
Registry.LocalMachine.OpenSubKey("SOFTWARE\Microsoft\Windows\Curr
entVersion\Uninstall\" &
Names.GetValue(y)).GetValue("DisplayVersion")
                If DisplayVersion Is Nothing = True Then
                    DisplayVersion = ""
                End If
                HelpLink =
Registry.LocalMachine.OpenSubKey("SOFTWARE\Microsoft\Windows\Curr
entVersion\Uninstall\" & Names.GetValue(y)).GetValue("HelpLink")
                If HelpLink Is Nothing = True Then
                    HelpLink = ""
                End If
                HelpTelephone =
Registry.LocalMachine.OpenSubKey("SOFTWARE\Microsoft\Windows\Curr
entVersion\Uninstall\" &
Names.GetValue(y)).GetValue("HelpTelephone")
                If HelpTelephone Is Nothing = True Then
                    HelpTelephone = ""
                End If
                InstallDate =
Registry.LocalMachine.OpenSubKey("SOFTWARE\Microsoft\Windows\Curr
entVersion\Uninstall\" &
Names.GetValue(y)).GetValue("InstallDate")
                If InstallDate Is Nothing = True Then
                    InstallDate = ""
                Else
```

```vbnet
                        InstallDate = Mid(InstallDate, 5, 2) & "/" &
Mid(InstallDate, 7, 2) & "/" & Mid(InstallDate, 1, 4)
                    End If
                    InstallLocation =
Registry.LocalMachine.OpenSubKey("SOFTWARE\Microsoft\Windows\Curr
entVersion\Uninstall\" &
Names.GetValue(y)).GetValue("InstallLocation")
                    If InstallLocation Is Nothing = True Then
                        InstallLocation = ""
                    End If
                    Publisher =
Registry.LocalMachine.OpenSubKey("SOFTWARE\Microsoft\Windows\Curr
entVersion\Uninstall\" & Names.GetValue(y)).GetValue("Publisher")
                    If Publisher Is Nothing = True Then
                        Publisher = ""
                    End If
                    UninstallString =
Registry.LocalMachine.OpenSubKey("SOFTWARE\Microsoft\Windows\Curr
entVersion\Uninstall\" &
Names.GetValue(y)).GetValue("UninstallString")
                    If UninstallString Is Nothing = True Then
                        UninstallString = ""
                    End If

            End If

        Next

    End Sub

End Class
```

And what that looks like:

Software\ODBC\ODBCINST.INI\ODBC Drivers

Name: Microsoft Text Driver (*.txt; *.csv)
Name: SQL Server
Name: Microsoft Excel Driver (*.xls)
Name: Microsoft ODBC for Oracle
Name: Microsoft Access Driver (*.mdb)
Name: Microsoft Paradox Driver (*.db)
Name: Microsoft dBase Driver (*.dbf)
Name: Microsoft Visual FoxPro Driver
Name: Microsoft FoxPro VFP Driver (*.dbf)
Name: Microsoft FoxPro Driver (*.dbf)
Name: SQL Server Native Client 11.0

Finally, the code for the 32-bit Provides:

```
Imports Microsoft.Win32

Public Class Form1

    Dim fso As Object =
CreateObject("Scripting.FileSystemObject")
    Dim txtstream As Object


    Private Sub Form1_Load(sender As System.Object, e As
System.EventArgs) Handles MyBase.Load

        'Providers
```

```
        fso = CreateObject("Scripting.FileSystemObject")
        txtstream = fso.OpenTextFile(Application.StartupPath &
"\Providers.html", 2, True, -2)
        txtstream.writeline("<hmtl>")
        txtstream.writeline("<head>")
        txtstream.writeline("<title></title>")
        txtstream.writeline("</head>")
        txtstream.writeline("<body style=""margin: 0px 0px 15px""
text=""#000000"" vlink=""#a89e89"" alink=""#a89e89""
link=""#c8c1b5"" bgcolor=""#ffffff"" leftmargin=""0""
topmargin=""0"" marginwidth=""0"">")
        txtstream.writeline("<center>")
        txtstream.writeline("<br>")
        txtstream.writeline("<br>")
        txtstream.writeline("<table>")
        txtstream.writeline("<tr><TH Nowrap STYLE=""FONT-
WEIGHT:normal; FONT-SIZE: 24px; COLOR: navy; FONT-STYLE: normal;
FONT-FAMILY: Times New Roman"">Windows Management
Experts  </TH></tr>")
        txtstream.writeline("<tr><TH Nowrap STYLE=""FONT-
WEIGHT:normal; FONT-SIZE: 48px; COLOR: navy; FONT-STYLE: normal;
FONT-FAMILY: Edwardian Script ITC"">System Management
Presentation Tools</TH></tr>")
        txtstream.writeline("<tr><TH Nowrap STYLE=""FONT-
WEIGHT:normal; FONT-SIZE: 12px; COLOR: DarkSlateGray; FONT-STYLE:
normal; FONT-FAMILY: font-family:Calibri, Sans-Serif"">" &
DateTime.Now & "</TH></tr>")
        txtstream.writeline("</table>")
        txtstream.writeline("</center>")
        txtstream.writeline("<br>")
        txtstream.writeline("<table cellpadding=1 cellspacing=1
width=100%>")


        Dim p As String = "clsid"

        txtstream.writeline("<tr><TH Nowrap colspan=2
STYLE=""FONT-WEIGHT:normal; FONT-SIZE: 18px; COLOR: black; FONT-
STYLE: normal; font-family:Calibri, Sans-
Serif;""><b><u>Discovered Providers</u></b></TH></tr>")


        Dim Names() As String =
Registry.ClassesRoot.OpenSubKey(p).GetSubKeyNames
```

```vbnet
        For x As Integer = 0 To Names.GetLength(0) - 1

            If Mid(Names.GetValue(x), 1, 1) = "{" Then
                Dim regkey As RegistryKey =
Registry.ClassesRoot.OpenSubKey("clsid\" & Names.GetValue(x) &
"\OLE DB Provider")
                If regkey Is Nothing = False Then
                    Dim value As String =
Registry.ClassesRoot.OpenSubKey("clsid\" & Names.GetValue(x) &
"\OLE DB Provider").GetValue("")
                    ComboBox1.Items.Add(value)
                End If
            End If

        Next


        For z As Integer = 0 To ComboBox1.Items.Count - 1
            txtstream.writeline("<tr>")
            txtstream.writeline("<th width=50% align=right Nowrap
STYLE=""FONT-WEIGHT:normal; FONT-SIZE: 12px; COLOR: DarkRed;
FONT-STYLE: normal; font-family:Times New
Roman;"">Name: </th>")
            txtstream.writeline("<td width=50% align=left Nowrap
STYLE=""FONT-WEIGHT:normal; FONT-SIZE: 12px; COLOR: navy; FONT-
STYLE: normal; font-family:Times New Roman;"">" &
ComboBox1.Items(z) & "</td>")
            txtstream.writeline("</tr>")
        Next


        WebBrowser1.Navigate(Application.StartupPath &
"\Providers.html")


    End Sub
End Class
```

And the view:

Discovered Providers

Name: Microsoft Jet 3.51 OLE DB Provider
Name: Microsoft Jet 4.0 OLE DB Provider
Name: Microsoft OLE DB Provider for Analysis Services 11.0
Name: Microsoft OLE DB Provider For Data Mining Services
Name: Microsoft OLE DB Provider for ODBC Drivers
Name: Microsoft OLE DB Provider for OLAP Services 8.0
Name: Microsoft OLE DB Provider for Oracle
Name: Microsoft OLE DB Provider for SQL Server
Name: Microsoft OLE DB Simple Provider
Name: MSDataShape
Name: OLE DB Provider for Microsoft Directory Services
Name: SQL Server Native Client 11.0

So, now, we switch to 64-bit.

The Provider Code:

```
Imports Microsoft.Win32

Public Class Form1

    Dim fso As Object =
CreateObject("Scripting.FileSystemObject")
    Dim txtstream As Object


    Private Sub Form1_Load(sender As System.Object, e As
System.EventArgs) Handles MyBase.Load

        'Providers
```

```vb
        fso = CreateObject("Scripting.FileSystemObject")
        txtstream = fso.OpenTextFile(Application.StartupPath &
"\Providers.html", 2, True, -2)
        txtstream.writeline("<hmtl>")
        txtstream.writeline("<head>")
        txtstream.writeline("<title></title>")
        txtstream.writeline("</head>")
        txtstream.writeline("<body style=""margin: 0px 0px 15px""
text=""#000000"" vlink=""#a89e89"" alink=""#a89e89""
link=""#c8c1b5"" bgcolor=""#ffffff"" leftmargin=""0""
topmargin=""0"" marginwidth=""0"">")
        txtstream.writeline("<center>")
        txtstream.writeline("<br>")
        txtstream.writeline("<br>")
        txtstream.writeline("<table>")
        txtstream.writeline("<tr><TH Nowrap STYLE=""FONT-
WEIGHT:normal; FONT-SIZE: 24px; COLOR: navy; FONT-STYLE: normal;
FONT-FAMILY: Times New Roman"">Windows Management
Experts  </TH></tr>")
        txtstream.writeline("<tr><TH Nowrap STYLE=""FONT-
WEIGHT:normal; FONT-SIZE: 48px; COLOR: navy; FONT-STYLE: normal;
FONT-FAMILY: Edwardian Script ITC"">System Management
Presentation Tools</TH></tr>")
        txtstream.writeline("<tr><TH Nowrap STYLE=""FONT-
WEIGHT:normal; FONT-SIZE: 12px; COLOR: DarkSlateGray; FONT-STYLE:
normal; FONT-FAMILY: font-family:Calibri, Sans-Serif"">" &
DateTime.Now & "</TH></tr>")
        txtstream.writeline("</table>")
        txtstream.writeline("</center>")
        txtstream.writeline("<br>")
        txtstream.writeline("<table cellpadding=1 cellspacing=1
width=100%>")


        Dim p As String = "SOFTWARE\Classes\CLSID"

        Dim Names() As String =
Registry.LocalMachine.OpenSubKey(p).GetSubKeyNames
        For x As Integer = 0 To Names.GetLength(0) - 1

            If Mid(Names.GetValue(x), 1, 1) = "{" Then
                Dim regkey As RegistryKey =
Registry.LocalMachine.OpenSubKey(p & "\" & Names.GetValue(x) &
"\Ole Db Provider")
                If regkey Is Nothing = False Then
```

```vb
                Dim value As String = regkey.GetValue("")
                If IsNothing(value) = False Then
                    ComboBox1.Items.Add(value)
                End If
            End If
        End If

    Next

    For z As Integer = 0 To ComboBox1.Items.Count - 1
        txtstream.writeline("<tr>")
        txtstream.writeline("<th width=50% align=right Nowrap
STYLE=""FONT-WEIGHT:normal; FONT-SIZE: 12px; COLOR: DarkRed;
FONT-STYLE: normal; font-family:Times New
Roman;"">Name: </th>")
        txtstream.writeline("<td width=50% align=left Nowrap
STYLE=""FONT-WEIGHT:normal; FONT-SIZE: 12px; COLOR: navy; FONT-
STYLE: normal; font-family:Times New Roman;"">" &
ComboBox1.Items(z) & "</td>")
        txtstream.writeline("</tr>")
    Next


    txtstream.writeline("</table>")
    txtstream.writeline("</th></tr>")
    txtstream.writeline("</table>")
    txtstream.writeline("</body>")
    txtstream.writeline("</html>")
    txtstream.Close()

    WebBrowser1.Navigate(Application.StartupPath &
"\Providers.html")


    End Sub
```

And the view:

Windows Management Experts

System Management Presentation Tools

6/27/2018 9:21:37 PM

Name: Microsoft OLE DB Provider for Analysis Services 11.0
Name: Microsoft OLE DB Provider for ODBC Drivers
Name: Microsoft OLE DB Provider for SQL Server
Name: Microsoft OLE DB Simple Provider
Name: MSDataShape
Name: OLE DB Provider for Microsoft Directory Services
Name: SQL Server Native Client 11.0

And the Drivers:

```
Imports Microsoft.Win32

Public Class Form2

    Private Sub Form2_Load(sender As System.Object, e As
System.EventArgs) Handles MyBase.Load


        Dim fso As Object =
CreateObject("Scripting.FileSystemObject")
        Dim txtstream As Object =
fso.OpenTextFile(Application.StartupPath & "\Drivers.html", 2,
True, -2)
        txtstream.writeline("<hmtl>")
        txtstream.writeline("<head>")
        txtstream.writeline("<title></title>")
        txtstream.writeline("</head>")
        txtstream.writeline("<body style=""margin: 0px 0px 15px""
text=""#000000"" vlink=""#a89e89"" alink=""#a89e89""
link=""#c8c1b5"" bgcolor=""#ffffff"" leftmargin=""0""
topmargin=""0"" marginwidth=""0"">")
        txtstream.writeline("<center>")
        txtstream.writeline("<br>")
        txtstream.writeline("<br>")
        txtstream.writeline("<table>")
```

```vb
        txtstream.writeline("<tr><TH Nowrap STYLE=""FONT-
WEIGHT:normal; FONT-SIZE: 24px; COLOR: navy; FONT-STYLE: normal;
FONT-FAMILY: Times New Roman"">Windows Management
Experts  </TH></tr>")
        txtstream.writeline("<tr><TH Nowrap STYLE=""FONT-
WEIGHT:normal; FONT-SIZE: 48px; COLOR: navy; FONT-STYLE: normal;
FONT-FAMILY: Edwardian Script ITC"">System Management
Presentation Tools</TH></tr>")
        txtstream.writeline("<tr><TH Nowrap STYLE=""FONT-
WEIGHT:normal; FONT-SIZE: 12px; COLOR: DarkSlateGray; FONT-STYLE:
normal; FONT-FAMILY: font-family:Calibri, Sans-Serif"">" &
DateTime.Now & "</TH></tr>")
        txtstream.writeline("</table>")
        txtstream.writeline("</center>")
        txtstream.writeline("<br>")
        txtstream.writeline("<table cellpadding=1 cellspacing=1
width=100%>")


        Dim p As String = "SOFTWARE\ODBC\ODBCINST.INI\ODBC
Drivers"


        txtstream.writeline("<tr><TH Nowrap colspan=2
STYLE=""FONT-WEIGHT:normal; FONT-SIZE: 18px; COLOR: black; FONT-
STYLE: normal; font-family:Calibri, Sans-Serif;""><b><u>" & p &
"</u></b></TH></tr>")


        Dim Names() As String =
Registry.LocalMachine.OpenSubKey(p).GetValueNames
        For x As Integer = 0 To Names.GetLength(0) - 1

            txtstream.writeline("<tr>")
            txtstream.writeline("<th width=50% align=right Nowrap
STYLE=""FONT-WEIGHT:normal; FONT-SIZE: 12px; COLOR: DarkRed;
FONT-STYLE: normal; font-family:Times New
Roman;"">Name: </th>")
            txtstream.writeline("<td width=50% align=left Nowrap
STYLE=""FONT-WEIGHT:normal; FONT-SIZE: 12px; COLOR: navy; FONT-
STYLE: normal; font-family:Times New Roman;"">" &
Names.GetValue(x) & "</td>")
            txtstream.writeline("</tr>")
        Next
        txtstream.writeline("<tr>")
```

```
txtstream.writeline("</table>")
txtstream.writeline("</th></tr>")
txtstream.writeline("</table>")
txtstream.writeline("</body>")
txtstream.writeline("</html>")
txtstream.Close()

WebBrowser1.Navigate(Application.StartupPath &
"\Drivers.html")


    End Sub

End Class
```

The View:

SOFTWARE\ODBC\ODBCINST.INI\ODBC Drivers

Name: SQL Server
Name: SQL Server Native Client 11.0

Registry naming conventions

I just realized that I didn't explain what some of the naming conventions mean.

According to my wife, I often take it for granted that the words I know that are being thrown around in the registry are familiar to you as they are to me.

Implemented Categories is where permission keys – such as safe for Initialization and safe for scripting are applied.

InProcHandler32 is short for in process handler which implies that this program supports OLE Automation.

InProcServer32 is short for In Process Server32 which implies that the program is activated using a dynamic link library or dll.

LocalServer32 is short for Local server 32 and implies that activation is based on using an exe.

ProgID is short for Programmatic Identifier. Excel.Application is a ProgID and you use it with createobject to create an instance of it.

VersionIndependentProgID is simply a ProgID without any numbers past the word that activates the program. For example, ADODB.Connection is a VersionIndependentProgID because the newest version – for example, ADODB.Connection.6.0 – may not be on other computers, making the VersionIndependentProgID a neutral call.

Typelib or Type Library – which is also in the registry – in the CLSID section helps you know there is a Type Library and the GUID that is the default value is where you will find the information about it in the TypeLib section of the registry. For example, HKEY_CLASSES_ROOT\TypeLib.

Control is a key that is used to help programs such as the ones in this book discover if the Object is a control or simply an object that can be created.

Controls generally have a user interface that allows the user to physically make changes and customize the use of the control.

Ole DB Provider is another registry key that is used to help programs and programmers know which entries in the registry are a specific kind of entry.

Again, we used this when we went searching for OLEDB Providers.

In Conclusion

I hope you have found this book to be useful. There is a lot of code here and samples of programs you can cut and paste into your own code. I wish you the best of luck.

www.ingramcontent.com/pod-product-compliance
Lightning Source LLC
Chambersburg PA
CBHW070856070326
40690CB00009B/1870